iOS

USER GUIDE

A Comprehensive Manual On How To Use The New iOS 18 With Tips And Tricks And Pictures For Beginners And Pro Users

By

Kelvin B. Smith

Table of Contents

INTRODUCTION

The IOS 18 was released alongside the iPhone 16 series and it comes with a lot of exciting features.

Personalize Your Home Screen

Personalize your Home Screen by resizing and arranging widgets and applications. Use the color picker on your iPhone or Tint to choose a hue that goes well with your background.

A Way To Secure And Hide Applications

Lock or hide important applications to protect the information they contain. To unlock an app that you've locked on your Home Screen, you'll need to enter your password, Face ID, or Touch ID. Put an app in a locked hidden applications folder and it will disappear from the Home Screen. When you lock or hide an app on your iPhone, its contents will not be visible in other areas of the device, including searches or notifications.

Modify The Lock Screen Keys

Alter the Lock Screen's bottom controls to include a timer or calculator.

Control Center

You can now access additional functions with the help of the reorganized Control Center, which includes new sets of controls. You can see all of your choices, including those from your preferred applications, in the controls gallery.

Photos

You can spend less time looking for images and more time appreciating them with the revamped Photos app. You may sort your images by a variety of categories, including Recent Days, Trips, People & Pets, and more. You may easily access the albums or collections that are most important to you by pinning them. You may personalize and enhance Photos to your liking by adjusting the app's settings.

Messages

Animate each letter, word, phrase, or emoji with a variety of effects, including bold, italics, underline, and strikethrough. Many of these effects are offered immediately as you write, so you can easily highlight your words. Use any sticker or emoji as a Tapback to respond creatively to communications. Keep in touch even when you're out of your cell phone or Wi-Fi range by setting a message to transmit at a later time and taking advantage of satellite capabilities.

The Safari

As you navigate, Safari will recognize important content and highlight it. Maps, translations, and connections to other resources may be seen in the highlights. To help readers quickly grasp the main points of an article, a revamped reader view now includes a table of contents and a high-level synopsis.

Password

One new app that can securely save your login information, verification codes, and passwords in one spot. The Passwords app will be immediately updated with all of your newly generated passwords when you utilize AutoFill.

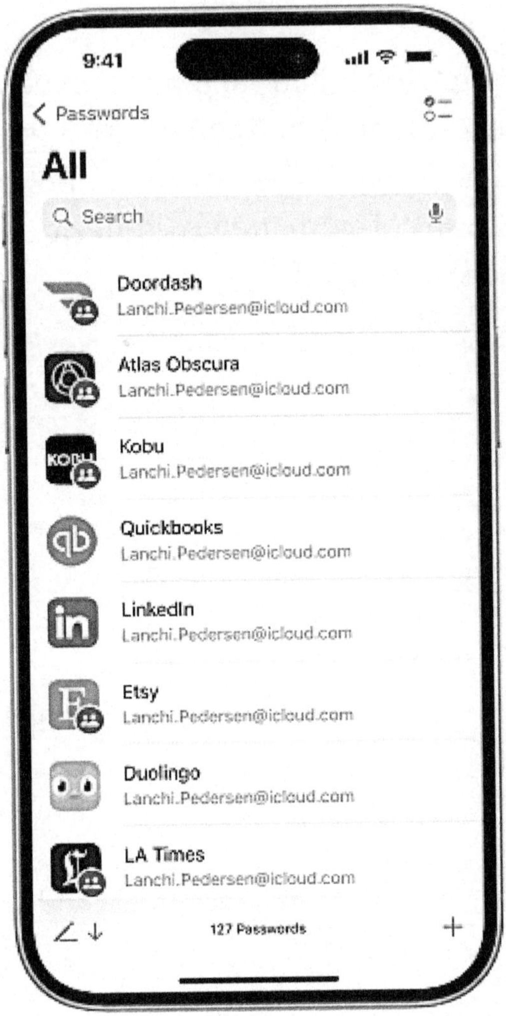

Road Maps

Explore all sixty-three national parks in the United States on topographic maps that include extensive hiking routes and trail networks. Easily access offline hiking maps with turn-by-turn audio navigation by saving them to your iPhone. With features including one-way, out-and-back, and loop routes, you may design your own walking and hiking paths.

FaceTime

Use your screen to show your friends and family how to use their gadgets by tapping and sketching. Otherwise, you need to get their OK before you may remotely use their equipment.

Wallet

Without exchanging phone numbers, you may use Tap to Cash to transfer and receive Apple Cash just by bringing your iPhone or Apple Watch close to another person's iPhone or Apple Watch. An event booklet detailing the location, along with app suggestions, is included with each ticket. With Apple Pay, you may see your reward or point balances in your Wallet and pay with them or in installments.

Notes

Transcribing spoken word into writing is as easy as recording it in a note. Math Notes allows you to quickly solve mathematical problems, utilize collapsible headers in sections with a lot of content, and make text stand out by adding color.

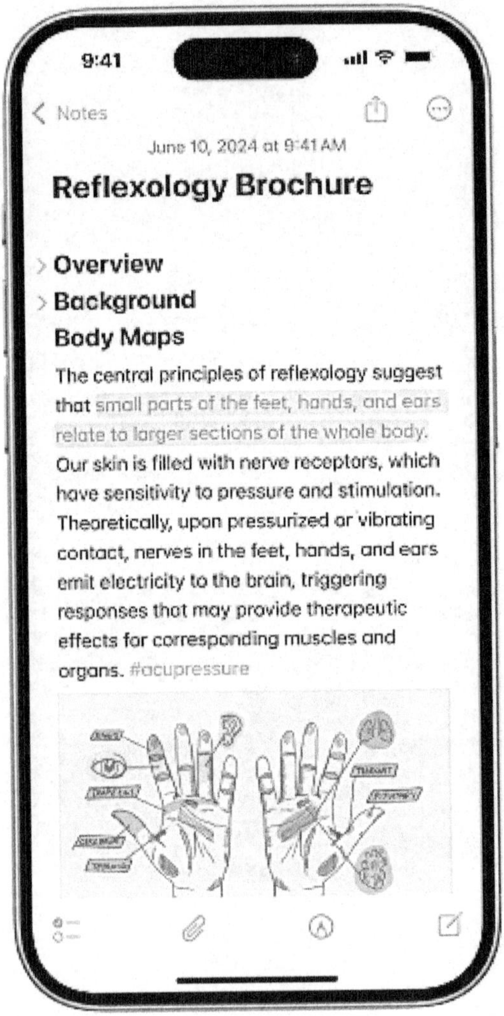

Journal

The Journal app keeps track of your mood, and the Health app counts the time you spend writing in it as mindful minutes. To stay on track with your journaling objectives, you may use the search function to locate and organize previous posts, as well as see your writing streaks and other statistics.

The Apple TV

Enhance Dialogue makes it easier to hear what's being said on screen, and InSight gives you additional information about the performers and music while a program or movie is playing.

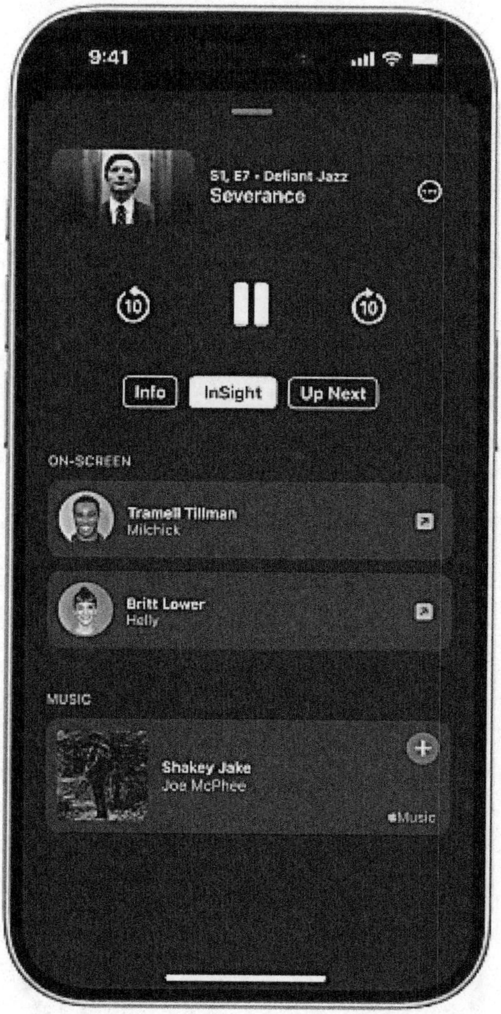

Home

Authorize visitors to use certain functions, such as garage doors, security systems, and door locks, on a prearranged basis.

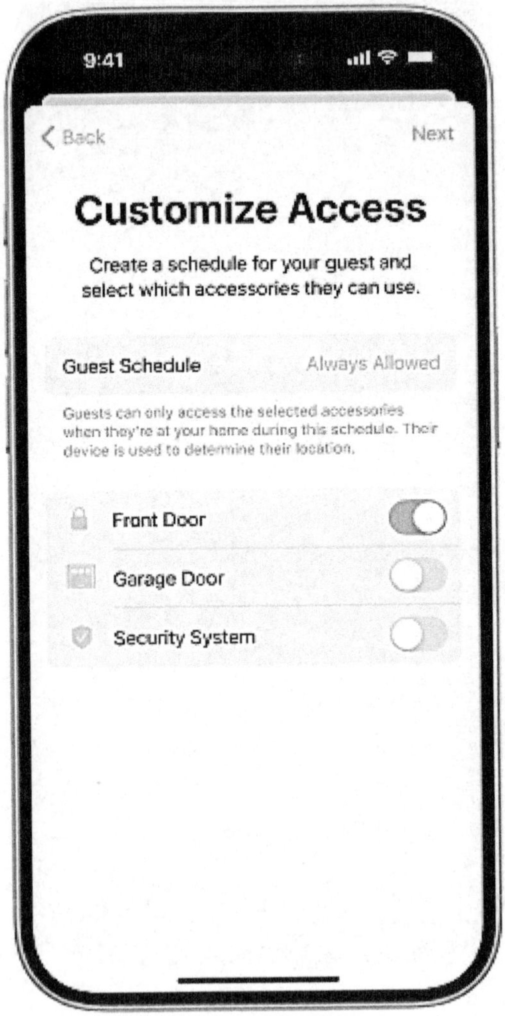

Security & Privacy

You can choose which contacts, rather than your full contact list, an app may access thanks to the revamped Privacy and Security settings, which also allow you to regulate the amount of information you share with applications.

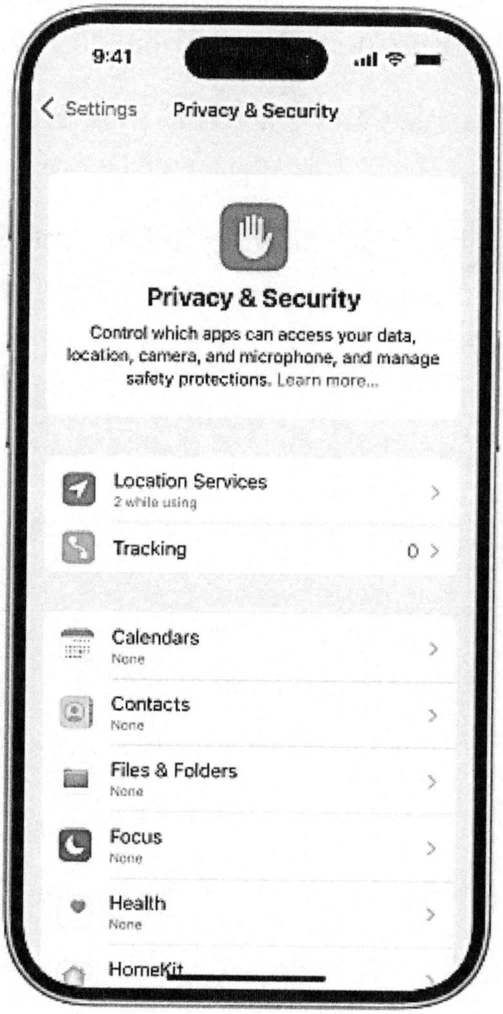

Accessibility

Thanks to Eye Tracking, users may now operate their iPhones just by looking at them. Vocal Shortcuts allow individuals with very unusual speech to record noises that initiate certain tasks on iPhone, while Music Haptics synchronizes the iPhone Taptic Engine with the beat of music.

Quick Response Live Video For Emergencies SOS

Get the support you need quicker and simpler by sharing streaming video and recorded media during emergency calls.

Freeform

You may show your board in sections using scenes. You may share your board with anybody by just sharing a link. Making connections on your canvas is now simpler with an updated diagramming mode.

Digital Calculator

Make use of modern resources, such as the ability to see past events and convert units. With Math Notes, you may evaluate equations, assign variables, create graphs, and much more—all by typing or handwriting the math.

Calendar

A revamped Month view streamlines the process of seeing the next month at a glance. Within Calendar, you'll find the Reminders app, which allows you to create, see, amend, and finish reminders.

Note: Apps and new features may not work on all iPhone models, regions, languages, or carriers.

CHAPTER ONE

HOW TO UPDATE YOUR IPHONE TO IOS 18

Make sure you have a backup of your vital data before installing any new software by backing up your device. Pick a backup plan.

Verify If Your iPhone Is Compatible.

Only updates that are compatible with the version of software you are now using will be shown to you. The option to install the most recent version will not be shown until you have downloaded it.

You may use iOS 18 on these iPhone models:

- iPhone 16
- iPhone 16 Plus
- iPhone 16 Pro

- iPhone 16 Pro Max
- iPhone 15
- iPhone 15 Plus
- iPhone 15 Pro
- iPhone 15 Pro Max
- iPhone 14
- iPhone 14 Plus
- iPhone 14 Pro
- iPhone 14 Pro Max
- iPhone 13
- iPhone 13 mini
- iPhone 13 Pro
- iPhone 13 Pro Max
- iPhone 12
- iPhone 12 mini
- iPhone 12 Pro
- iPhone 12 Pro Max
- iPhone 11
- iPhone 11 Pro
- iPhone 11 Pro Max
- iPhone XS
- iPhone XS Max
- iPhone XR
- iPhone SE (2nd generation or later)

Update Your iPhone Automatically

You have the option to set your iPhone to automatically update while it charges overnight.

Follow these steps to enable automatic updates:

1) Go to Settings menu, tap General then click Automatic Update.
2) Locate the option to enable automatic installation and download of iOS updates, and then turn it on.

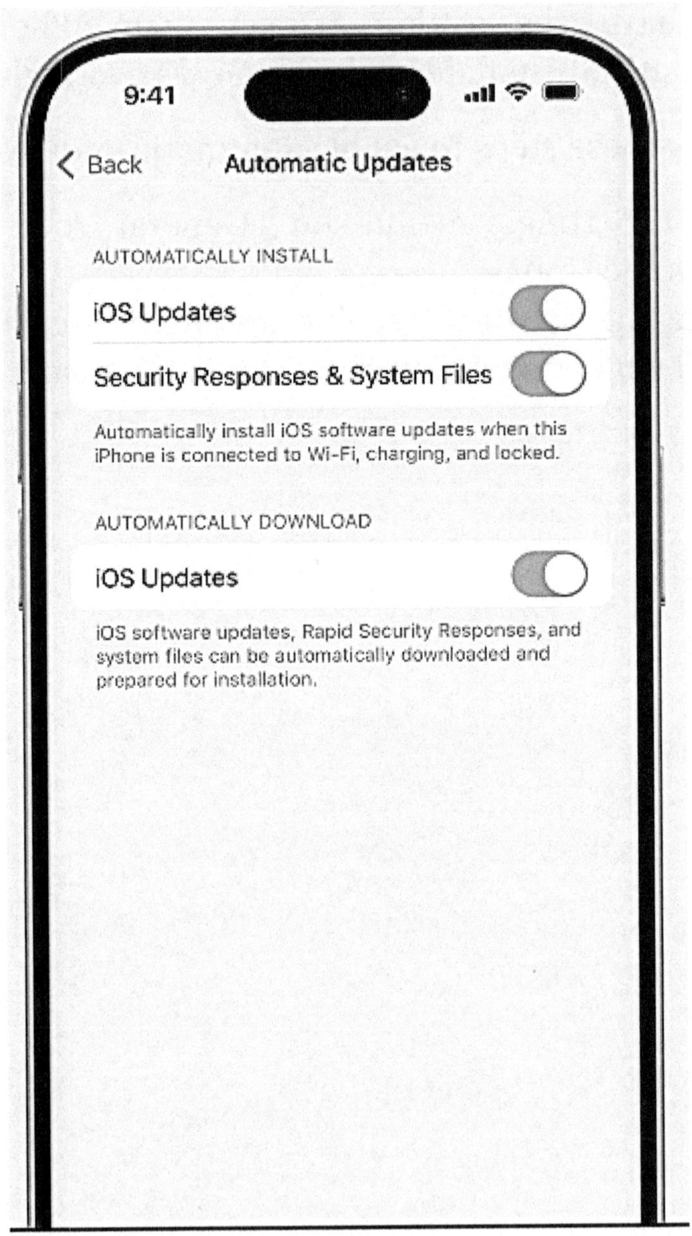
9:41
Back
Automatic Updates
AUTOMATICALLY INSTALL
iOS Updates
Security Responses & System Files
Automatically install iOS software updates when this iPhone is connected to Wi-Fi, charging, and locked.
AUTOMATICALLY DOWNLOAD
iOS Updates
iOS software updates, Rapid Security Responses, and system files can be automatically downloaded and prepared for installation.

While plugged into a power source and Wi-Fi, an iPhone will automatically download and install any available updates. Before installing an update, you will get a notification.

Navigate to Settings > General > Software Update > Automatic Updates to disable automatic updates.

Update Your iPhone Wirelessly

1) Use iCloud or your PC to create a backup of your device.
2) Plug your iPhone in and link it up to Wi-Fi.
3) Go to Settings > General then press Software Update.
4) Select the desired software update from the list if more than one is shown.

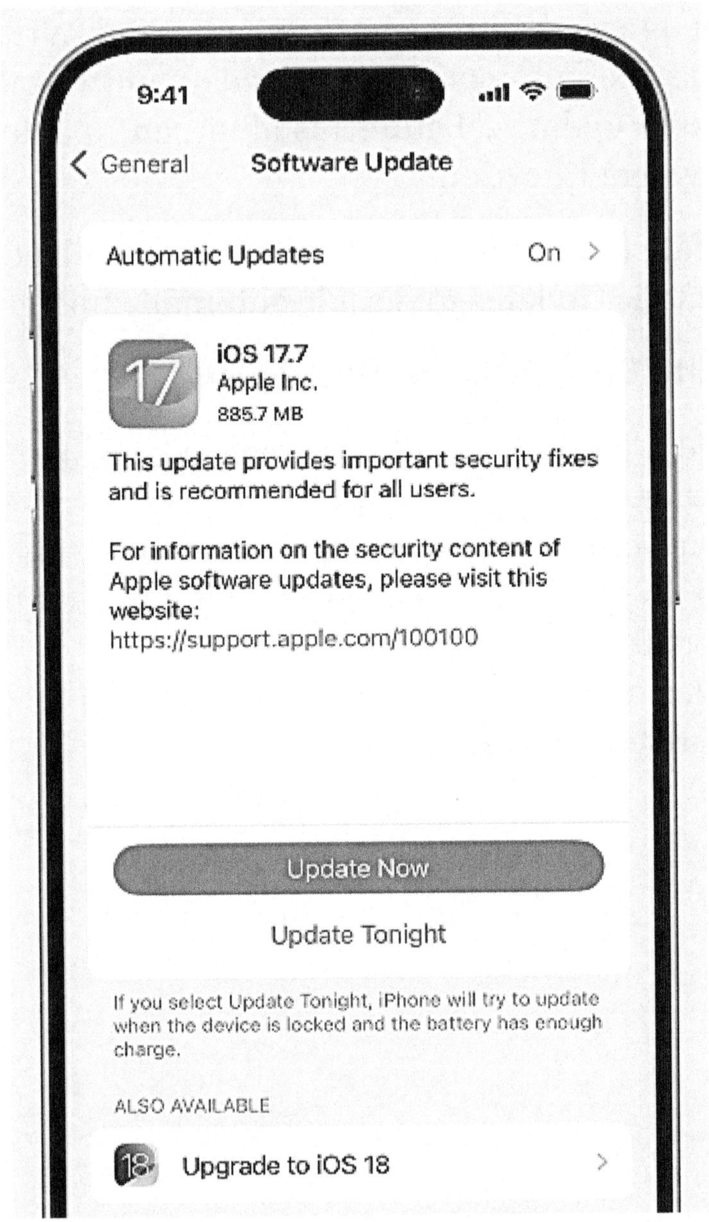

5) Click on the "Install Now" button. To install the update, input your passcode, and download it.

Note: You can't always get the latest software upgrades wirelessly. Your device may be unable to connect to the update servers if you are using a VPN or proxy connection.

If More Space Is Required When Upgrading Wirelessly

When prompted, press Continue to enable the temporary removal of applications. This is necessary to make room for software updates. Those applications are reinstalled automatically after installation is finished. To manually remove stuff from your device to create more space, choose Cancel instead.

HOW TO POWER ON AND SET UP YOUR IPHONE ON IOS 18

1) Start Up Your Ios Device

Press and hold the power button on your smartphone until it brings up the Apple logo, It will then display "Hello" in many languages. To begin, just follow the directions that appear on the screen.

The Hello screen is where you may use VoiceOver or Zoom, which can help those with poor eyesight or no vision at all.

2) Customize The Font And Icon Size On Your iPhone

Choose from Default, Medium, and Large to set the font and icon sizes to your liking. You may preview the chosen choice by swiping the icon between those sizes; the text and graphics on this Appearance screen will change accordingly.

When you're satisfied with the size, drag the icon to the one you want and hit Continue.

3) Choose Quick Start And Manual Setup

Quick Start allows you to automate the setup process of your new device when you have another device nearby.

Select "Set Up Without Another Device" if you're not using any other devices.

Accessibility Options may be configured by tapping the blue button.

4) Activate Your IOS Device

To activate and proceed with the setup of your device, you must establish a connection to a Wi-Fi or cellular network.

Choose a Wi-Fi network to connect to, or, if none is available, choose "Continue Without Wi-Fi" to use the cellular data plan on your smartphone. You may be required to enter your SIM card into your iPhone or iPad before setting up Wi-Fi + Cellular on your iOS device. Additionally, you may be prompted to activate your eSIM.

5) Set Up For You Or Your Little One

Go on to the next step and choose whether you or a youngster will be setting up your iPhone.

6) Set Up Your Fingerprint Or Face ID And Make A Passcode

To enable fingerprint or facial recognition to unlock your phone and pay for things, follow the on-screen prompts to set up Touch ID or facial ID.

To further secure your information, use a six-digit passcode. Passcodes are required for the usage of Apple Pay, Face ID, and Touch ID. Select Passcode Options to set your passcode type: four digits, bespoke, or none at all.

7) Get All Of Your Data And Applications Back Or Transferred

Pick the method you like for transferring or restoring data from one device to another. You may transfer data from an Android smartphone, use an iCloud backup, or import a backup from your PC.

Avoid transferring apps and data if you don't own a backup or another device.

8) Use Your Apple ID Or A Different Apple Device To Log In

After that, type in the password that you use to access your Apple Account, which may be either an email or a phone number. Or choose "Forgot password or don't have an Apple Account?" You may establish an Apple Account, change your password, or access your existing one from that page.

Select Other Sign-In Options, and then choose Use Multiple Accounts, if you're using more than one Apple ID.

A verification code from an old device may be requested when you log in with your Apple Account.

9:41
Back
Apple Account
Sign in with an email or phone number to use iCloud, the App Store, and other Apple services.
Email or Phone Number
Forgot password or don't have an account?
Your Apple Account information is used to enable Apple services when you sign in, including iCloud Backup, which automatically backs up the data on your device in case you need to replace or restore it. Your device serial number may be used to check eligibility for service offers. See how your data is managed...
Continue
Other Sign-In Options

9) You May Configure Various Features And Enable Automatic Updates

When prompted, follow the on-screen prompts to enable automatic software updates for iOS or iPadOS and to configure additional capabilities, such as cellular data, a phone number, or Apple Pay:

- Services and features, such as Siri, will need your setup or activation. For Siri to recognize your voice, you may be required to say a few sentences on some devices.
- Then, to set up Screen Time, which will show you and your children how much time is spent on various gadgets, follow the on-screen instructions. You may also restrict how much time you spend using the app each day.
- The next step is to find out what information you can provide Apple and decide if you want to give app developers access to it.
- At last, choose Light or Dark to get a sneak peek at your iPhone's changes. To set your iPhone to alternate between the two modes automatically while you're using it, tap the Auto button. Press Continue when you are ready to finish.

CHAPTER TWO

HOW TO CUSTOMIZE THE IOS 18 HOME SCREEN

The Home Screen widgets and app icons may have their colors changed, tints applied, sizes adjusted, and app names removed.

1) Access the Home Screen.
2) Press and hold the backdrop of the Home Screen until you see the icons start to wiggle.
3) Select Customize after tapping Edit in the upper-right corner of the screen.
4) Perform one of these tasks:

- **Make Icons Larger:** Select Large. (When you enlarge the image, the app names will not display.)
- **You May Give Widgets And Icons A Dark Or Bright Look:** Select Dark or Light from the options. By selecting Automatic, you may make the icons and widgets look darker at night and lighter during the day.
- **Icons And Widgets May Have Their Colors Changed:** Select Tinted. Color and saturation may be adjusted using the sliders. Additionally, the eyedropper may be used to choose a color for your icon background.

9:41
Messages
Calendar
Photos
Camera
App Store
Small
Large
Automatic
Dark
Light
Tinted
Add a color tint
to the icons.

HOW TO CUSTOMIZE WIDGETS ON IOS

To Begin With, What Exactly Are Widgets?

You may quickly and easily see today's news, weather, reminders, battery life, and more with the help of widgets. To make this information always accessible, you may see widgets in Today See and then add them to your Home Screen or Lock Screen.

You can access a variety of widgets—including those for Music, Podcasts, Safari, Home, Contacts, and more—on the Home Screen or Lock Screen without ever launching the app. To play a song or podcast, for instance, just hit the Play button on the widget corresponding to that category.

Tip: A Smart Stack (the one with the dots next to it) is a collection of widgets that use data like time, location, and activity to show you the most relevant widget at the right moment based on your day. You may access the widgets included in a Smart Stack by adding them to the Home Screen from the widget gallery and swiping them up and down.

Integrate A Widget Onto Your Home Screen

1) Access the Home Screen.
2) Tap and hold the Home Screen background until the applications start to wiggle. Then, locate the Home Screen page where you want to install the widget.
3) To access the widget gallery, press Edit located at the top of the screen. Then, hit Add Widget.
4) Locate a widget by scrolling or searching, press it, and then use the sliders to adjust the size.

Information is shown differently by the various sizes.

5) Select the desired size, and then press the Add Widget button.
6) You may drag the widget to the desired location on the screen while the applications continue to wiggle, and then hit the Done button.

Make Use Of Widgets

Widgets on the Home Screen, Lock Screen, or StandBy may be used to execute operations. With a simple touch, you can cross an item off your To-Do list in the Reminders widget, play an episode in the Podcasts widget, or even switch on the lights in your living room—all without launching an app.

Edit Widget On The Home Screen

You may change the data shown by most widgets from the Home Screen to suit your needs. If you're using a Mail widget, for instance, you may scroll down to the mailbox it displays, touch on it, and then choose another mailbox to have its messages shown in the widget. Smart Stacks also lets you personalize the way they cycle among widgets depending on factors like your current activity, location, time of day, and more.

1) Access the Home Screen.
2) The fast actions menu may be accessed by touching and holding a widget.
3) Select choices by tapping Edit Widget (or Edit Stack, if it's a Smart Stack).

You can manage widgets in a Smart Stack in a few different ways: you may toggle Smart Rotate and Widget Suggestions (located below the widget) on or off, rearrange them within the stack by dragging and dropping, relocate them to the Home Screen from the Smart Stack, or delete them all by hitting the Remove button on the top left.

By enabling Widget Suggestions, your Smart Stack will be automatically updated with widgets for applications you use often, taking into account your previous actions. To make the widget readily available whenever you need it, you may add it to your stack using an option.

4) Press the Finish button.

TAKE A WIDGET OFF THE MAIN SCREEN

1) Access the Home Screen.

2) The fast actions menu may be accessed by touching and holding the widget.

3) Choose an option from these:

- You may remove a widget by tapping on the removed widget.
- Hit the Remove Stack button to remove the Smart Stack.

Observe Widgets In Today's View

Swipe right from the left side of the Home Screen and then scroll up and down to browse widgets in Today Browse.

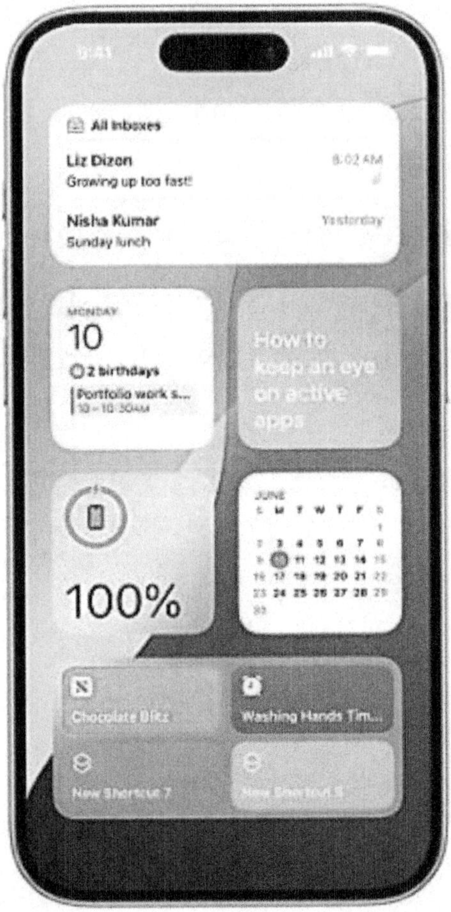

Explore Widgets In Today View And Search When iPhone Is Locked

1) To enable Face ID and Passcode on an iPhone equipped with Face ID or Touch ID and Passcode on an older iPhone model, go to the Settings menu.

2) Your passcode is required.

3) After you've enabled Allow Access When Locked, you'll see Today View and Search.

HOW TO PERSONALIZE YOUR LOCK SCREEN ON IOS 18

A lot of customization options are available for your Lock Screen, including wallpaper, picture display, time font, widgets, and more.

You can create many Lock Screens, toggle between them, and even associate a Lock Screen with a Focus. You may, for instance, choose a separate Lock Screen for use when you're at your desk.

Set Up A Custom Lock Screen

1) To access the iPhone's Lock Screen, double-press the side button.
2) Press and hold the Lock Screen until the buttons to Personalize and Add New show up at the screen's bottom.
   If your passcode prompts don't show up, try touching and holding the Lock Screen again.
3) To create a new Lock Screen, hit the Add New button. To edit an existing Lock Screen, slide to the screen you want to update, select Customize, and then tap Lock Screen.

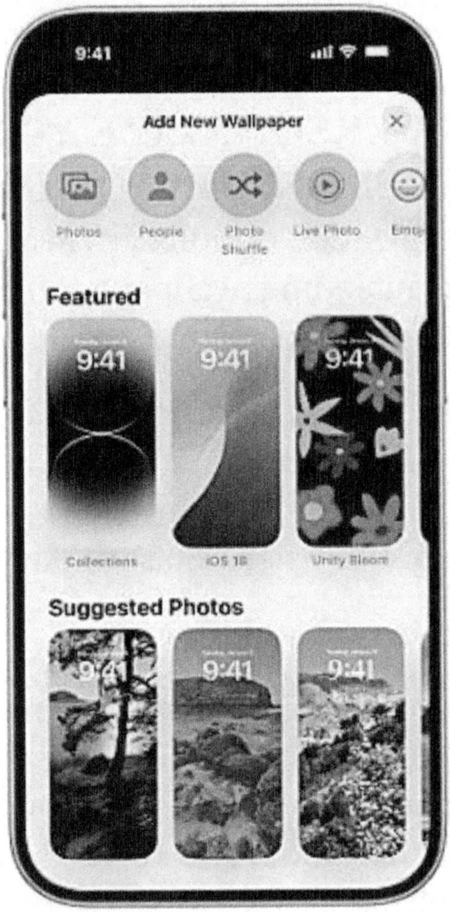

4) Pick a wallpaper from the gallery to use as your Lock Screen when making a new one.

5) To alter the style, color, and font, tap the time.

6) Tap on Add Widgets, the date, or the field under the time to include widgets that display information like today's news, the weather, and calendar events.

7) Select an option by tapping the Add or Done button:
   - Select The Wallpaper You Want To Use For Both The Home Screen And The Lock Screen: Use the Set as Wallpaper Pair option.
   - You May Customize The Home Screen Even Further: Select Home Screen Personalization.

To make the applications pop, you may alter the wallpaper color, use a custom picture by tapping the picture On the Rectangle button, or blur the wallpaper by selecting Blur.

Personalize The Lock Screen Clock

The clock on your lock screen may have its typeface and color changed.

1) To access the iPhone's Lock Screen, double-press the side button.

2) Press and hold the Lock Screen until the buttons to Personalize and Add New show up at the screen's bottom.

If your passcode prompts don't show up, try touching and holding the Lock Screen again.

3) To edit a Lock Screen, swipe to it, hit Customize, and then select the picture you want to use.

4) Once you've tapped the time, choose a typeface and color.

You may adjust the weight of the typeface (available for solid fonts) by dragging the slider.

MODIFY THE LOCK SCREEN'S CONTROLS LOCATED AT THE SCREEN'S BASE

If you're shopping or traveling, you may switch out the Lock Screen controls for the Calculator or the Translate app, for example. On top of that, you can customize each Lock Screen with its own set of options or even disable them altogether.

Tip: You may alter the Lock Screen's bottom controls to your liking and then associate them with a certain Focus.

1) To access the iPhone's Lock Screen, double-press the side button.

2) Press and hold the Lock Screen until the buttons to Personalize and Add New show up at the screen's bottom.

If your passcode prompts don't show up, try touching and holding the Lock Screen again.

3) After selecting Customize, choose Lock Screen.

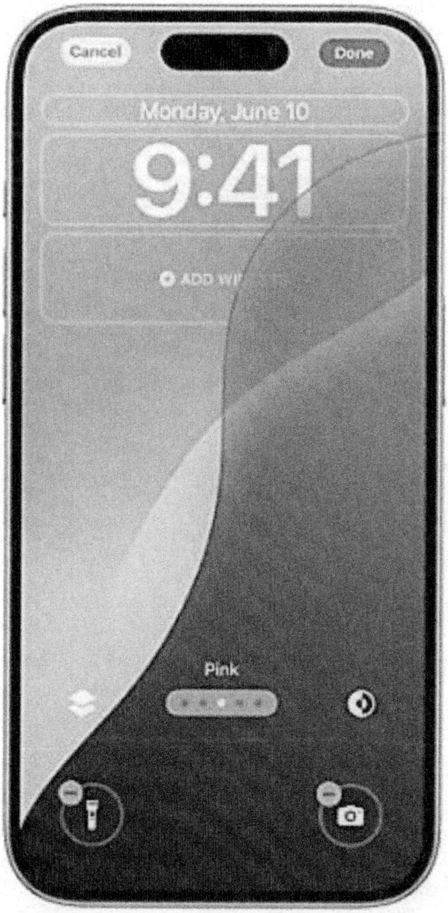

4) After selecting a control from the list at the screen's bottom and tapping the Remove button, you may access the controls gallery by tapping the Add Quick Action button.

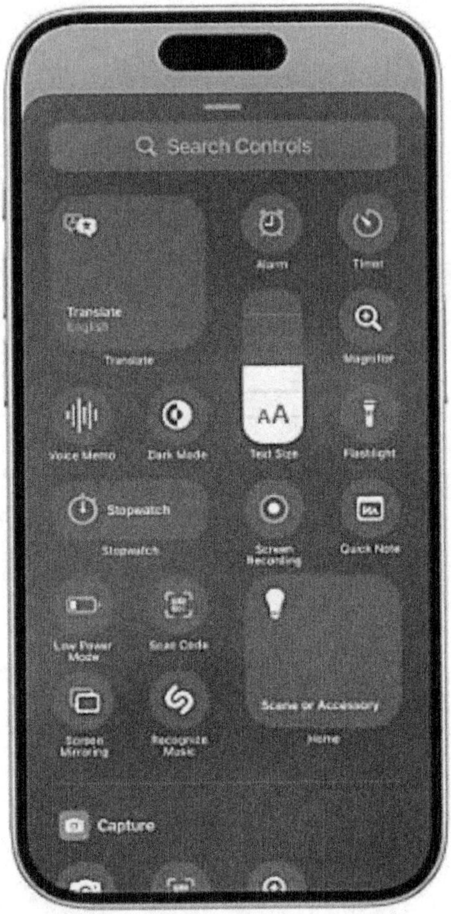

5) Choose a new lock screen control from the controls gallery by tapping on it.

6) Tap Done at the top of the screen, then tap the Lock Screen, after you complete changing the controls at the bottom of the screen.

HOW TO MAKE YOUR UNIQUE LOCK SCREEN PICTURE

Selecting an image to use as your Lock Screen gives you a lot of customization options, like moving it around and altering its look.

Perform one of these tasks:

- Rearrange Your Photo: To rearrange your picture, use the pinch-open gesture to zoom in, the drag-and-drop gesture with two fingers to move it, and the pinch-closed gesture to zoom out.
- Alter The Photo Style: To experiment with various picture effects, you may swipe left or right to access a variety of typefaces and color filters.
- Create A Multilayered Effect: If your picture allows for layers, such as one with people, dogs, or the sky, you may create a multilayered effect by tapping the More button in the lower right corner and selecting Depth Effect.

  Note: Only supported models have access to the multilayered effect. When the topic is too far away, too high, or too obstructive of the clock, layering may not be an option.

- Make A Live Photo With Motion Effect: To make a Live Photo, choose one that can be slowed down by tapping the Play button on the bottom left. Then, when your smartphone wakes up, the Live Photo will start playing.
- Change The Shuffle Frequency: If you pick Photo Shuffle, you'll be able to get a preview of the images by hitting the Browse button. To change the shuffle frequency, hit the More button, and then choose an option under Shuffle Frequency.

Tip: You may use your photo library to immediately add a picture on the Home Screen and the Lock Screen. To share an image from the Photos app, open the Library, choose an image, and then hit the Share button. After you find "Use as Wallpaper" in the navigation bar, touch "Add," and then decide whether you want it to appear on the Home screen or the Lock screen.

Link A Focus To A Lock Screen

Reduce interruptions and stay focused on what you're doing with the aid of focus. To temporarily block all alerts or only those that are relevant to your current job, you may configure a Focus. Any time you utilize a certain Lock Screen that you've linked to a Focus, your Focus settings will be automatically applied.

1) To access the iPhone's Lock Screen, double-press the side button.
2) To access the Customize option, press and hold the Lock Screen until it shows up at the screen's bottom.
3) To access the Focus settings, such as Do Not Disturb, Personal, Sleep, and Work, tap Focus at the wallpaper's bottom.

Note: Make sure to go to Settings > Focus to set up a Focus if you don't see it toward the bottom of your wallpaper.

4) After you've chosen a focus, hit the Close button.

Edited Or Changed The Lock Screen

You may make changes to your personalized Lock Screen after you've created it.

1) To access the iPhone's Lock Screen, double-press the side button.
2) To access the Customize option, press and hold the Lock Screen until it shows up at the screen's bottom.

If the Lock Screen doesn't show up, try touching and holding it again, and then enter your passcode.

3) Tap Customize, then tap Lock Screen when you swipe to the screen you want to modify.

4) Perform one of these tasks:
   - Modify The Clock's Style, Color, And Font: Select the time.
   - Include Today's News, The Forecast, And Upcoming Events In the Widget Form: Select the area under the clock, the date, or tap on Add Widgets.
   - Change The Wallpaper: Hit on Done, then on the Add New option. Select a wallpaper, and hit Add. After that, pick either Set as Wallpaper Pair or Customize Home Screen as your new wallpaper.

Choose Between Different Lock Screens

You have the option to create many personalized Lock Screens and toggle between them as the day progresses.

1) To access the iPhone's Lock Screen, double-press the side button.

2) To access the Customize option, press and hold the Lock Screen until it shows up at the screen's bottom.
3) To access your preferred Lock Screen, just swipe to it and press on it.

Note: If a Lock Screen is associated with a certain Focus, moving it to a different Lock Screen will also change your Focus.

HOW TO REMOVE A LOCK SCREEN

If you don't need a lock screen anymore, you may remove it.

1) To access the iPhone's Lock Screen, double-press the side button.
2) To access the Customize option, press and hold the Lock Screen until it shows up at the screen's bottom.
3) To remove a Lock Screen, just slide up on the screen until you reach it, then hit the Trash icon. From there, choose Delete This Wallpaper.

CHAPTER THREE

HOW TO USE THE CONTROL CENTER ON THE OS 18

A variety of helpful functions, such as Airplane Mode, Do Not Disturb, flashlight, volume, screen brightness, and more, are conveniently located in the iPhone's Control Center.

Open Control Center

Choose one of these options to launch the Control Center:

- If your iPhone is equipped with Face ID, you may unlock it by swiping down from the top right corner.
  By dragging the icons down the right side of the screen, you may access different sets of controls. Return to the first set by swiping up through the icons.

Use the up-arrow gesture from the screen's center bottom to dismiss Control Center.

- Swipe from the bottom to the top on an iPhone that has a Home button. You may access other sets of controls by swiping them up.
  Just hit the Home button to dismiss the Control Center.

Use Control Center To Access More Controls

Extra choices are provided via several controls. Press and hold a control to see its choices. Control Center allows you to accomplish things like:

- Press and hold the set of controls located in the upper left corner of the screen. Then, to access the AirDrop settings, press the button.
- To capture a picture, video, or selfie, press and hold the Camera button.

Personalize The Control Center

In Control Center, you can rearrange, add, or delete controls.

1) Open the Control Center.

2) To start customizing the controls, tap the Add button located in the upper left corner of the Control Center.

3) Perform one of these tasks:

- Rearrange Controls: Drag a control to a different location to rearrange them.
- Remove control: On the control's top left, you should see the Remove button; tap on it.

- Resize Controls: You may resize controls by dragging the handle located at the bottom right of each control.
- Add More Control Button: You may access the controls gallery by tapping the Add a Control button on the screen's bottom. From there, you can tap on a control to add it to the Control Center.

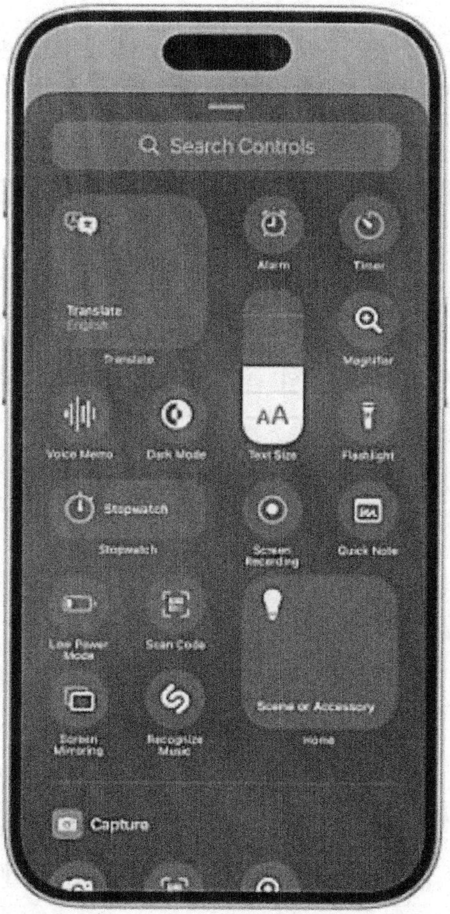

4) When you're done configuring, swipe up from the center bottom of the screen to dismiss Control Center.

Add A Custom Set Of Controls

The Control Center may accommodate additional sets of controls.

1) Open Command Center.

2) To add an item, use the plus sign in the upper left corner.

3) Select the symbol located at the very bottom of the screen—the little circle—on the right side of the screen.

4) Press the Add a Control button located at the screen's footer to access the controls folder.

5) To include a control in the group, touch it in the controls gallery.

6) Any of the following may be done to further personalize the new set of controls:

- Drag a control to a different location to rearrange them.
- Uninstall a single control or a few: On the control's top left, you should see the Remove button; tap on it.
- Controls may be resized by dragging the handle located in the control's bottom right corner.
- To access the controls gallery, hit Add a Control at the Control Center's bottom. From there, you may tap on another control to add it to the group.

7) When you're done configuring, swipe up from the center bottom of the screen to dismiss Control Center.

HOW TO DISABLE ACCESS TO THE CONTROL CENTER IN APPS

To disable Access Within Apps, go to Settings > Control Center.

HOW TO USE THE NOTIFICATION CENTER ON THE IOS 18

Make sure you're getting alerts the way you want them to and see and control them to reduce distractions.

Launch From The Locks Screen

When you pick up your iPhone or wake up your iPad, you may view your latest notifications on the Lock Screen. From the Lock Screen, you may also accomplish the following:

- Select an alert and tapping on it will launch the app from whence it came.
- Selecting several alerts at once brings up all of the most recent alerts for that particular app.
- You may modify app alerts or remove a notice by swiping leftover it.
- If the app provides it, you may examine the notice and take rapid action by touching and holding it.

Navigate to Settings > Notifications > Show Previews, and then choose Always to see notification information on the Lock Screen without unlocking your mobile.

Notifications may be seen even while your iPhone is in StandBy mode, starting with iOS 17 and later.

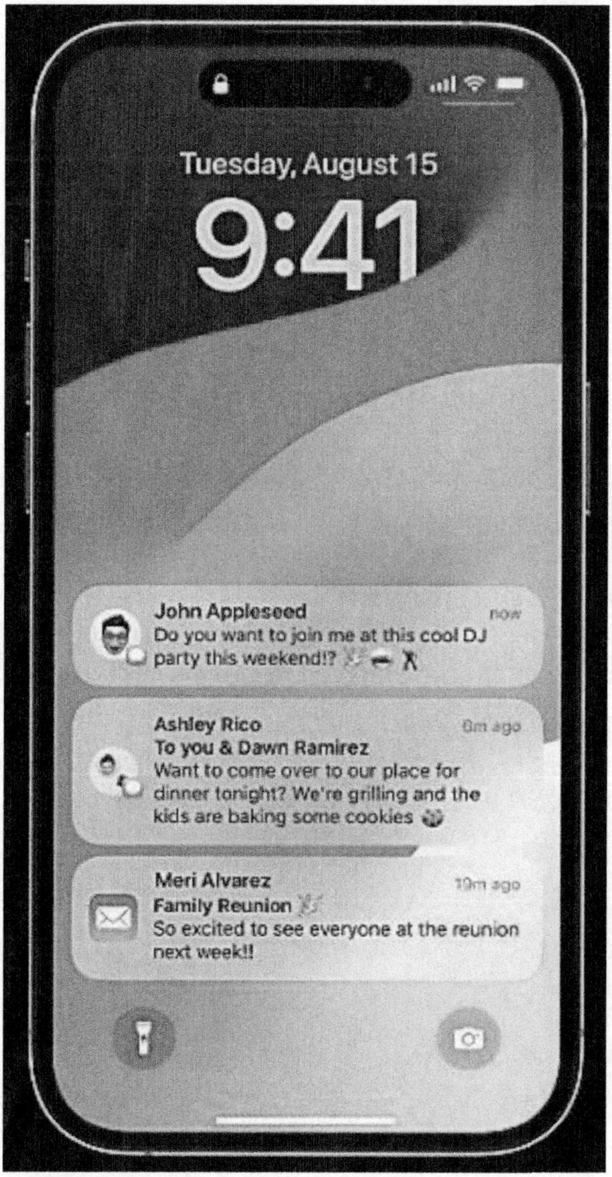

Open The Notifications Center

You may see all of your missed alerts in the Notification Center by scrolling back through your history. The Notification Center provides two methods to see your alerts:

- Swipe up from the center of the screen on the lock screen.
- Swipe down from the upper left corner of your screen, even while you're on another screen.

Press the Close button, then choose Clear to erase all of your notification history.

Organize Notification

From the Lock Screen or the Notification Center, you may manage your notifications:

1) To dismiss an alarm or set of notifications, swipe left.

2) Pick one of these choices after tapping Option:
   - Keep Off for One Hour
   - Mute for Today
   - View Settings
   - Turn Off

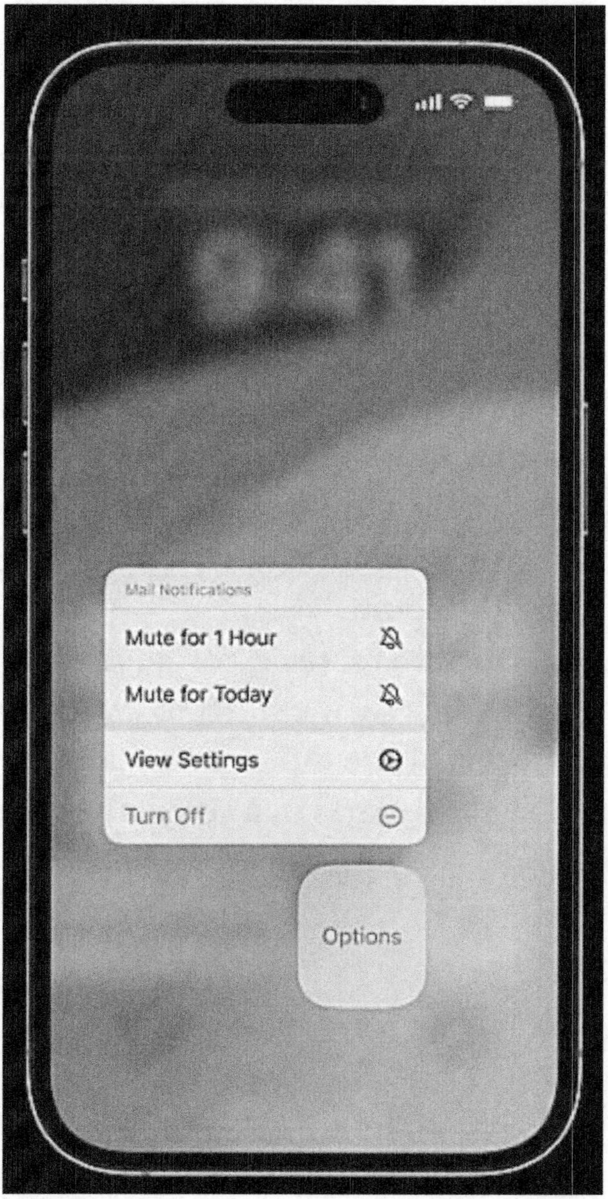
Mail Notifications
Mute for 1 Hour
Mute for Today
View Settings
Turn Off
Options

To customize your alert style or modify the settings for a particular app, you can also tap on View Settings.

HOW TO MODIFY THE APPEARANCE OF NOTIFICATION

1) Find Notifications in the Settings menu.
2) To customize the appearance of notifications on the Lock Screen, go to Display As and choose:
   - Count: Bottom of the screen, you'll see the count, which displays the total number of notifications. Notifications may be accessed by tapping the count.
   - Stack: Displays a series of alerts horizontally across the screen, starting with the most current one at the top.
   - List: Displays alerts in a sequential list.

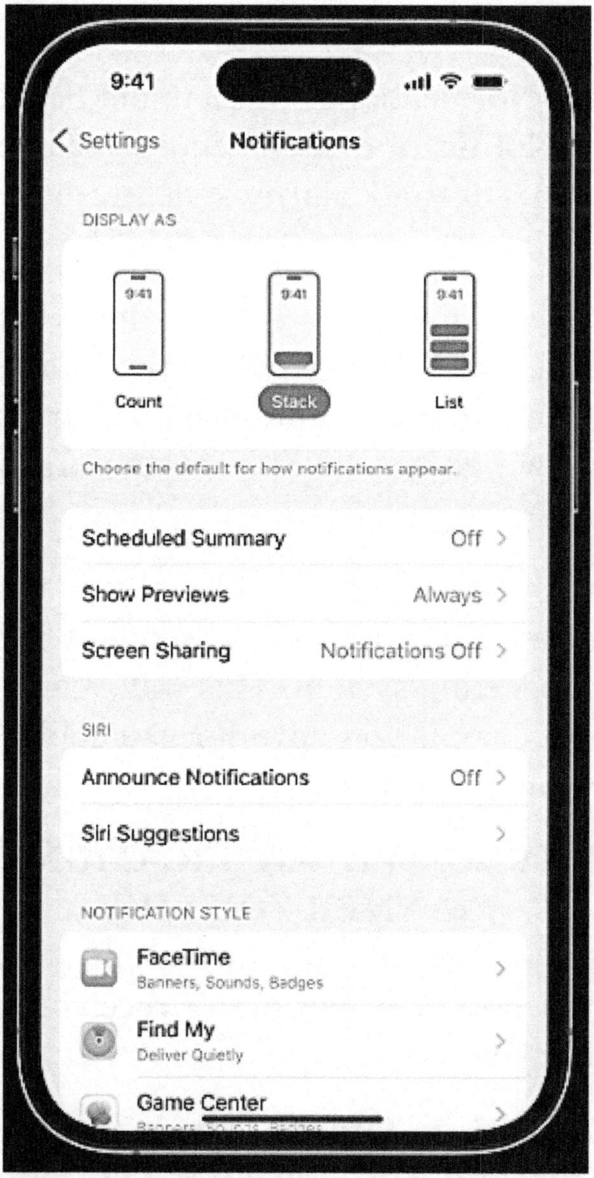

Note: To modify the appearance of your notifications, you must have iOS 16 or a later version.

Modify The Styles Of Notification

1) Find the Notifications option under Settings.
2) Under "Notification Style," choose an app.
3) Select the desired alarm style from the Alerts menu.

Some app icons may show information when badges are enabled. For instance, when you enable badges for Mail, the number of unread emails in your inbox will be shown above the Mail button on the Home Screen.

You may enable Critical Alerts for compatible applications in iOS 15 and subsequent versions of the iPad operating system. This way, alerts will still be received even if you have Focus enabled or your iPhone is muted.

HOW TO RECEIVE NOTIFICATION IN THE MANNER YOU LIKE

You may have accidentally turned off or enabled a notification option if you aren't receiving alerts in the manner you like.

A Focus Option That Minimizes Alerts May Be Customized And Activated Or Deactivated

Focus is a feature included in iOS 15 and subsequent versions of iPadOS that allows you to remain in the present when you need to focus or put down your smartphone. You may adjust the settings of Focus to get alerts and notifications at certain times and from specific applications or contacts.

1) Open the Command Center.
2) When the Focus option, such as Work or Do Not Disturb, displays, tap on it. (The Focus indicator alone indicates that the Focus option is not active.)
3) For the second time, tap the Focus option to disable it.

Get Notification From The Apps You Want

1) Go to the Settings app and touch on alerts.
2) Select the app from which you have not yet received any alerts.
3) You may customize the how and where you get notifications by turning on the option to Allow Notifications.

Depending on your preference, you may configure alerts to show up on the Lock Screen, in the Notifications Center, or as a Banner while you're using your iPhone.

Siri will read aloud app alerts when you enable Announce alerts.

HOW TO FIND AND USE APPS IN THE APP LIBRARY ON IOS 18

Sorted into sections like "Social," "Entertainment," and "Productivity & Finance," your applications are shown in the App Library. To make finding and using your most frequently used applications a breeze, they are conveniently located at the very top of their respective categories and right at the top of the screen.

Note: The applications in the App Library are intelligently categorized according to your app use. Although you may pin applications from the App Library to the Home Screen, rearranging them inside the App Library is not possible.

Navigate And Launch An App In The App Library

1) From the Home Screen, swipe left to access the App Library after you've gone through all the Home Screen pages.
2) To find an app, go to the top of the screen and tap the search bar. Type in the app's name. The alphabetical list may also be accessed by scrolling up and down.
3) Pressing on an app launches it.

You may access all the applications in a category by tapping on its little app icons.

How To Show Or Hide Home Screen Pages

You may not need as many Home Screen pages for applications now that you can locate them all in the App Library. App Library is now conveniently located near your initial Home Screen page, thanks to the ability to conceal specific Home Screen pages. (The buried pages may be seen again if desired.)

1) Press and hold the Home Screen wallpaper on the Home Screen until you see the app icons wiggle.
2) Pull down the menu to the very bottom of the screen.

You may see thumbnails of the sites on your Home Screen with checkmarks underneath them.

3) By tapping to remove the checkmarks, you may hide pages.

You may add checkmarks to reveal hidden pages by tapping on them.

4) If you're using Face ID on your iPhone, tap Done; otherwise, hit the Home button.

After you hide the other Home Screen pages, swiping left or right will take you directly to the App Library (and back again).

Note: You may find that new applications you download from the App Store end up in your App Library rather than the Home Screen when you hide the Home Screen sections.

Reorder Page On The Home Screen

The sequence of the Home Screen pages may be changed. As an example, you may create a Home Screen page that has all of your favorite applications and then set it as your primary Home Screen.

1) Press and hold the Home Screen wallpaper on the Home Screen until you see the app icons wiggle.

2) Pull down the menu to the very bottom of the screen.

You may see thumbnails of the sites on your Home Screen with checkmarks underneath them.

3) Press and hold any page on the Home Screen to reposition it, and then drag it.

4) For iPhones that have Face ID, double-tap the Done button. For iPhones without Face ID, press and hold the Home button twice.

Modify The Location of the app. Download

Upon purchasing an app from the App Store, you have the option to add it to either the Home Screen and the App Library, or only the App Library.

1) For the Home Screen and App Library, go to Settings.

2) Press either the Add to Home Screen or the App Library Only button.

Note: Be sure to toggle Show in App Library if you want app notification badges to show up in the App Library.

HOW TO TRANSFER AN APP FROM THE APP LIBRARY TO THE HOME SCREEN

You may simply restore an app's Home Screen placement after transferring it to the App Library.

1) Go to the App Library.

2) To bring an app to the Home Screen, press and hold it until its icons start to wiggle, and then release your finger.

CHAPTER FOUR

HOW TO USE GESTURES ON THE IOS 18

Although it may take some practice, being proficient with the iPhone's navigation gestures can greatly improve the efficiency and comfort of your regular interactions with the device. However, a large portion of the user base is still in the dark about a few of the most effective and efficient gestures.

Whether you're an old hand at using iPhones or just starting, these little techniques will make your smartphone so much better. Whether you're navigating between applications or just want to reach the controls with a swipe, these six motions will make your life easier.

1) Get Back To The Top

You can quickly return to the top of your iPhone's display by tapping the status bar located at the top of the screen whether you're in Safari or scrolling through a lengthy app menu or feed.

When the Dynamic Island isn't active, pressing it on an iPhone 14 Pro, iPhone 15 and iPhone 16 models does the same thing.

2) Switching Application

On iPhones that don't have a Home button, you may quickly access previously used applications with the Quick App Switcher. This functionality eliminates the need to launch the app switcher screen completely. If you often move between apps, such as while transferring data, this is the way to go.

A simple horizontal swipe over the bottom edge of your iPhone's screen will do the trick. With only a swipe of your finger, you may access any of your previously used applications.

3) Speed Up Camera Access

To make sure you never miss a photo while capturing memories on camera, this iPhone camera function is meant to work quickly and spontaneously.

To access the camera on your locked iPhone, just wake up the screen and swipe left instead of clicking the camera icon. The Camera app is instantly launched, so you may start taking images or movies, as soon as you do this.

4) Uncover The Secret Trackpad

It may be frustrating to use your iPhone to navigate and edit text, particularly when you need to put the cursor exactly where you want it. Luckily, there's a secret Apple function in the virtual keyboard that can fix this.

When you write something longer and realize you made a mistake, you may easily undo it by long-pressing the space bar. This will turn the on-screen keyboard into a touchpad, allowing you to manage the cursor with ease. Quickly and easily move the pointer to any location in your text with this feature.

You may also pick portions of text by tapping the trackpad with another finger while in this mode.

With these two features, customizing text on your iPhone is a snap. You should try it the next time you write a letter or message.

5) Search Spotlights

Quickly locate everything on your iPhone, from applications and contacts to emails and online results, with the help of Spotlight Search. It's a strong and efficient function. Thanks to Apple's Live Text function, Spotlight can even search text in your images.

Just slide down the center of the screen from any home screen. By doing so, you'll bring up the Spotlight Search bar and a keyboard to input your search query at the top of your screen. The Lock Screen is just another way to access it. (Under the "Allow Access When Locked" menu option, you may deactivate Today View and Search, which can be found in Settings CAN Face ID & Passcode.)

6) Reachability

Especially on bigger versions, the reachability feature of the iPhone makes it simpler to operate with one hand. You may access the top-level icons, buttons, and other items without using both hands by momentarily dragging the top half of the screen down.

Go to Settings FS Accessibility CAN Touch to activate the function, and then toggle the switch next to Reachability to on. Then, delicately drag the bottom edge of the screen (the part above the Home button on iPhone SE models or the gesture bar on models without a Home button) downwards to activate the feature. With a simple drag, the whole screen will descend, making the top part more accessible. Simply repeating the motion will bring the screen back to its full size.

HOW TO SEARCH WITH SPOTLIGHT ON THE IOS 18

You can use Live Text on your iPhone to search for text in images, contacts, and even content in applications like Mail and Messages. All across your system and the web, you may access stock and currency data, as well as locate and launch websites, applications, and photos in your picture library.

App shortcuts for your next probable activity display inside the Top Hit when you search for an app. (When you look for Photos, for instance, a shortcut to the Favorites album shows up.)

You can choose which applications to include in search results under Settings > Search. As you enter, search changes results and provides recommendations depending on how you use the app.

Choose Which Applications To Add To Search

1) Go to the settings menu, then click on Search.
2) Find an app, touch it, and then toggle the Show App in the Search switch.

Use The iPhone To Search

1) If your model has Face ID, you can find the Search button at the very bottom of the Home Screen. If not, you may also slide down from either the Home Screen or the Lock Screen.
2) Use the search bar to enter your search terms.
3) Perform one of these tasks:
- To begin searching, use the Search or Go button.
- Launch a recommended app: Press on the app.
- Move swiftly: Timer activation, Focus activation, music name retrieval via Shazam, shortcut execution, and much more are all at your fingertips. You may use the Shortcuts app to find existing shortcuts for apps or to make your own. Just search for the app's name.

- View a recommended online resource: Hit it.
- Find out additional details about a search suggestion: After that, you may access it by tapping one of the results.
- Begin a fresh search: Click the button that says "Clear Text" next to the search bar.

Disable Location-Based Suggestion

1) Locate Location Services in the Settings menu, then choose Privacy & Security.
2) To disable Suggestions & Search, go to System Services and tap OK.

Search Within Apps

A search bar or button is a common feature in applications that allows users to quickly locate what they're looking for. One example is the ability to search for a particular place in the Maps app.

1) Use the app's search bar or the Search button to search.

   Sliding down from the top should reveal a search bar if none is visible.
2) Choose a search term and hit the Search button.

Add A Dictionary

You may utilize dictionaries on your iPhone to improve your search capabilities.

1) Go to the Settings menu, click General then find Dictionary.
2) Choose a dictionary.

HOW TO USE THE MESSAGE APP ON IOS 18

Apple's Messages app is getting a makeover in iOS 18, with improvements including improved messaging with green bubble people, updated effects, improved formatting, Tapback response adjustments, satellite support, and a slew of amusing Apple Intelligence enhancements.

Learn about all the updates and additions to the Messages app in iOS 18, as well as what's on the horizon, with this comprehensive guide.

HOW TO USE SEND LATER

One new feature in iOS 18 is the ability to set a future date and time for an iMessage to be delivered. For instance, you may prepare a happy birthday SMS message in advance if you know someone's birthday is approaching.

When chatting with other iMessage users, you can schedule a message; but, when messaging with an Android user, you will not have this option. Assuming everyone involved has an Apple device and can use iMessage, it works in both one-on-one and group conversations.

Just follow these instructions to schedule a message:

1) Start a discussion using the Messages app.
2) To the left of the text field, you should see a "+" button; tap on it.
3) Press the More button.
4) Pick the option to Send later.
5) Enter your message here.
6) Click on the blue bubble that says Tomorrow at 9:00 am to adjust the send time. Next to it, you'll see a slider that allows you to enter the current date and time.
7) Once you've chosen a time and entered your message, you may schedule it by tapping the blue arrow.

If today is August 1, for instance, you have until August 15 to plan a message. This window of opportunity is available up to 14 days in advance. Even when your iPhone doesn't have a data or Wi-Fi connection, messages will still be sent.

At the very bottom of every chat, you'll see any scheduled messages. Press the "Edit" button to modify or delete a message's scheduled delivery time. The timing, deletion, and instant sending of the message are all customizable choices.

HOW TO USE TAP-BACK REACTIONS

When you long-press on a message, you may utilize the small characters known as tapbacks to react. This way, you can avoid typing out a lengthy response when a thumbs up or heart would do. Two major changes have been made to Tapbacks in iOS 18.

Redesigned Layout

More complexity and color have been added to the six basic Tapback icons. Both the new appearance and the ability to react by long-pressing on texts and receiving tapbacks are visible.

In a group conversation, you can now see who sent what when you touch on a Tapback you've got on a message. This is important for when you get numerous Tapback answers.

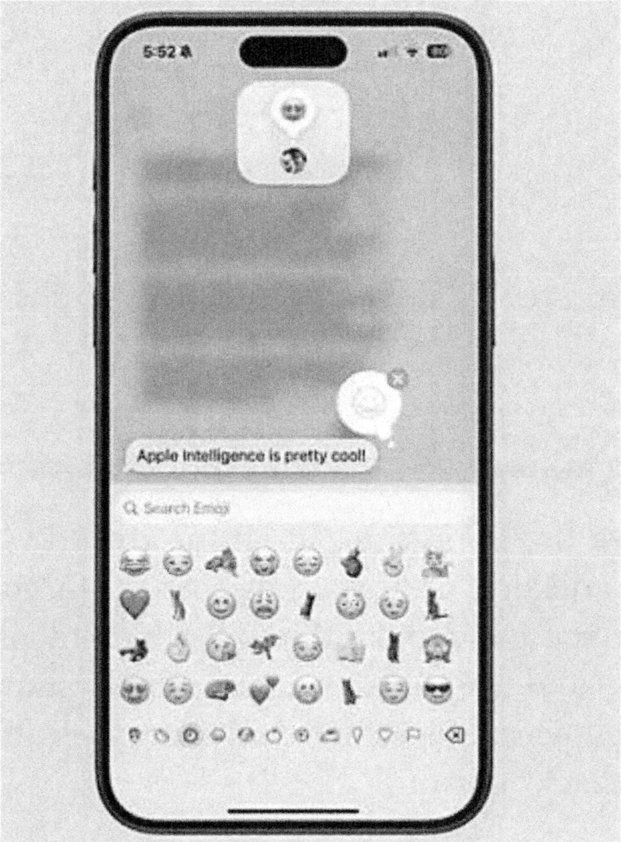

Emoji Compatibility

Now you may choose any emoji character while using Tapback, in addition to the six conventional ones. You can see typical emoji answers by swiping to the left after long pressing on a message, or you can access the emoji picker by tapping the generic emoji symbol thinking bubble.

You have the option to pick from a wide variety of emojis, stickers, and Memojis. At the bottom left, you'll notice two icons: Memoji, which takes you to Memoji, and the sticker icon, which shows your sticker choices. Select one and then press the "Add as a Tapback" button.

Stickers may not be easily legible on a Tapback, however Memoji and most emoji characters should be OK.

HOW TO USE RICH COMMUNICATION SERVICES (RCS)

Rich Communication Services (RCS) is an alternative to Multimedia Messaging Service (MMS) and Short Message Service (SMS). If the person you are messaging doesn't have iMessage, such as an Android user, you will see this. Though it enhances communications with green bubble Android users, RCS has zero bearing on iMessage conversations—those with other Apple device owners, represented by blue bubbles.

RCS is a more up-to-date technology than SMS, enabling better feature parity in discussions across Android and iPhone via text messaging. A lot of the problems you may have had with texting on an

Android smartphone, such as failing to transfer media files, are fixed with RCS.

The benefits of RCS are as follows:

- Enhanced picture and video quality.
- Allows for the transfer of bigger files and their support.
- Messages in audio format.
- Typing indications that work in real-time.
- View the receipts.
- Capability to send messages over cellular or Wi-Fi (SMS is just for cellular). Sending an RCS message over Wi-Fi does not incur any fees.
- Enhanced group conversations.

Rest assured, RCS is only applicable when conversing via text with an Android user. The blue and green bubbles aren't going anywhere, and iMessage is still the go-to for chats between Apple devices.

COMMUNICATIONS VIA SATELLITE

Messages by satellite is an innovative new feature that utilizes the same satellites used by Apple for the Emergency SOS via satellite function. It allows you to send messages even without a Wi-Fi or cellular connection.

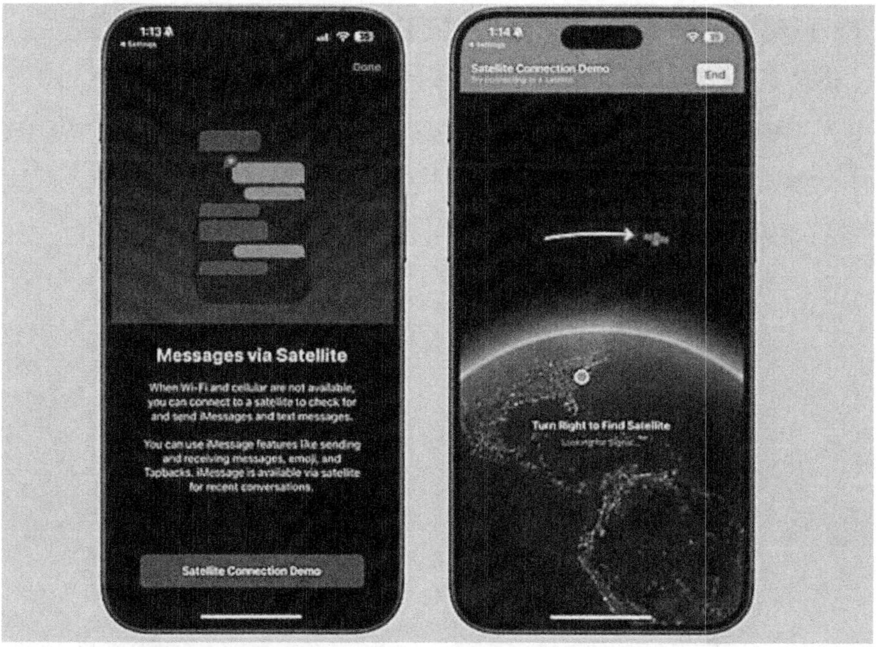

You aren't confined to messaging just with other iPhone users when you utilize Messages via satellite, which is accessible on iPhones 14 and later. You may send and receive both iMessage and SMS messages.

Similar to Emergency SOS by satellite, Messages via satellite are now free. Along with the two years of free satellite access that comes with an iPhone 14 or later, Apple has extended the free access period for the iPhone 14 until November 2025. When asked about the potential price of satellite connectivity, Apple has remained tight-lipped.

HOW TO USE SMART REPLIES (APPLE INTELLIGENCE AVAILABLE IN IOS 18.1)

To help you respond quickly to messages, your iPhone may use Apple Intelligence to evaluate the text and provide Smart Reply alternatives.

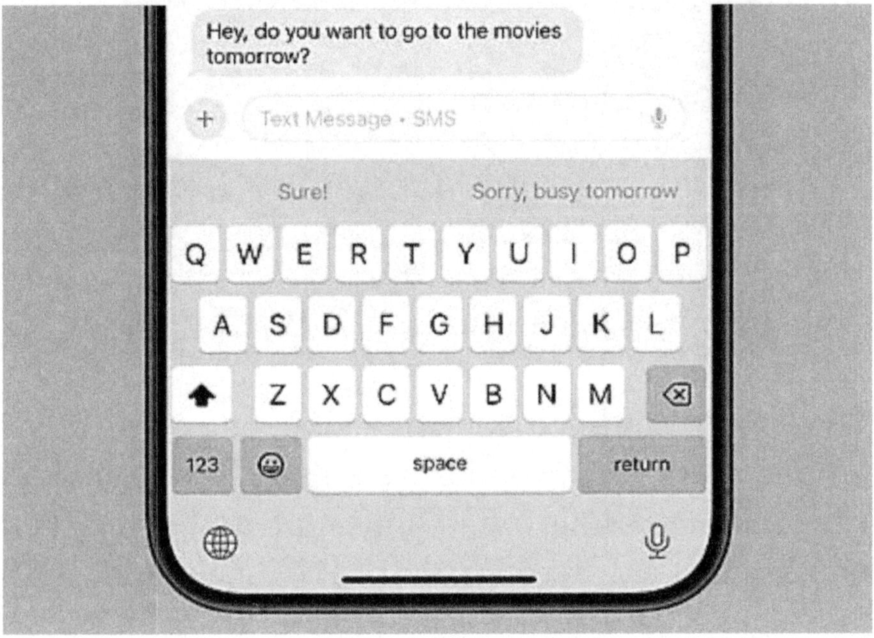

If you get a message from someone asking you a question like "Do you want to go to the movies?" Your message may have suggested a response such as "Sure!" or "Sorry, busy tomorrow." Not every message you receive will have the option to use Smart Replies, but Apple usually provides a recommendation.

Similar to how recommendations appeared in earlier iOS versions, Smart Replies now sit above the keyboard. Instead of just word recommendations that appear as you write, Smart Replies are more sophisticated and often include whole sentences and answers.

Simply tapping on a Smart Reply will bring up the text box where you can type it out. You may just disregard the advice and provide your answer if you choose not to. Ignoring a Smart Reply won't prevent you from seeing recommendations.

HOW TO USE WRITING TOOLS (APPLE INTELLIGENCE AVAILABLE IN IOS 18.1)

The Writing Tools feature is available anywhere you can type text, not only in the Messages app. One way to access the Writing Tools interface in Messages is to enter some text and then use the tap-and-drag motion to select it.

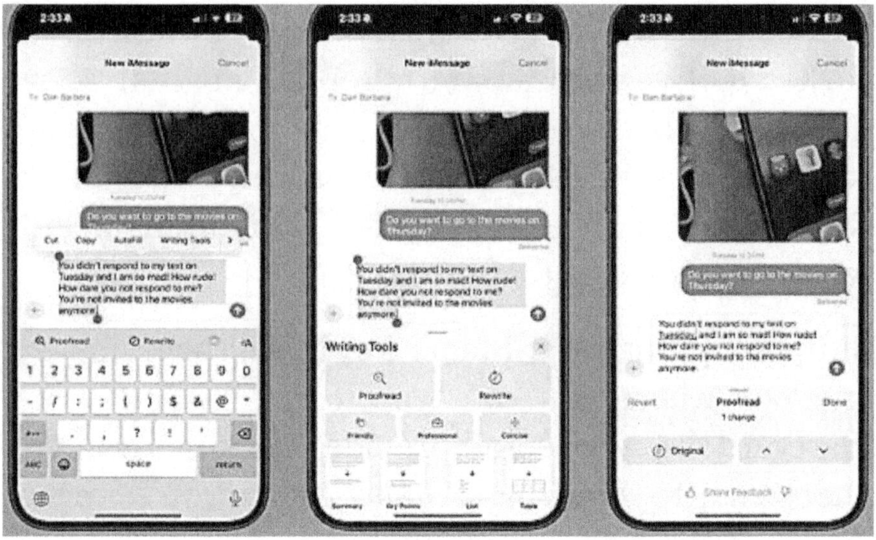

Some things that Writing Tools can do with a text message are:

- Make sure that what you've written is error-free in terms of grammar, spelling, word choice, and sentence structure by proofreading it.
- Alter the tone of your writing by selecting between Friendly, Professional, or Concise.
- Provide a brief overview of your work. You have the option to generate a table, extract important points, compile a list of subjects, or get a summary.

The Writing Tools are accessible via a series of menus; after modifying, you may see it in preview mode and either keep it or replace it with your text.

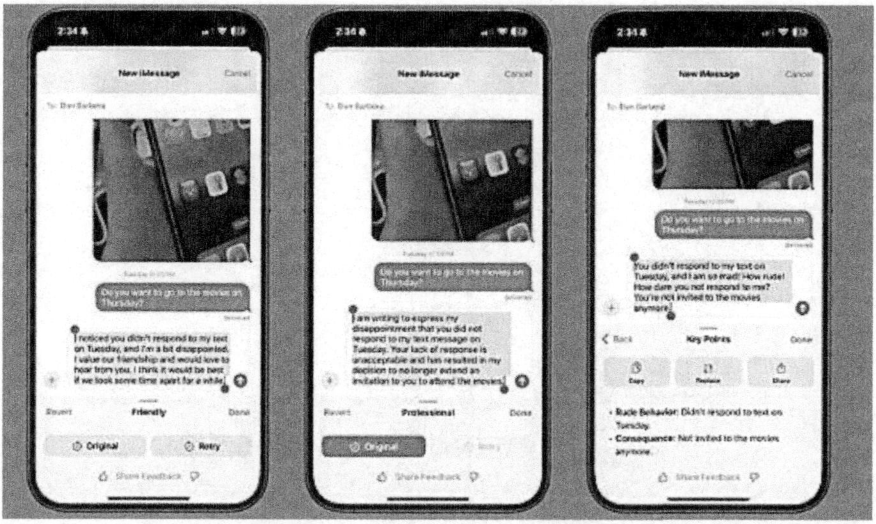

HOW TO USE OVERVIEW OF NOTIFICATION (APPLE INTELLIGENCE AVAILABLE IN IOS 18.1)

If the Messages app has sent you more than one notice, Apple Intelligence will condense them for you. This way, you can quickly scan them and focus on the most relevant ones.

This applies to both one-on-one and group chats, and the summaries will be shown on the lock screen. With iOS 18.1, you'll be able to see summary notifications.

HOW TO USE EMOJI DESIGN

In iOS 18, a single emoji is sent to the recipient with a significantly bigger appearance, making the information easier to perceive. Even when using different amounts of emojis, their size remains constant.

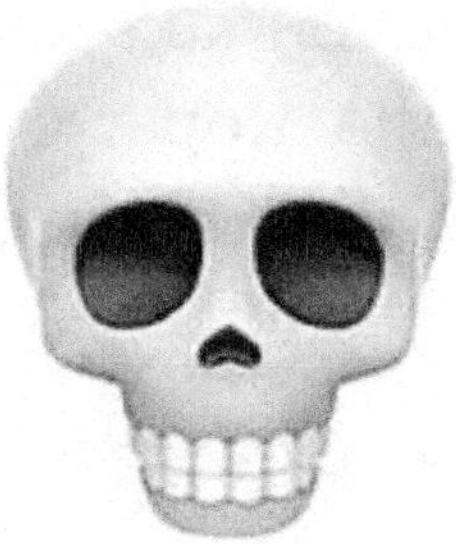

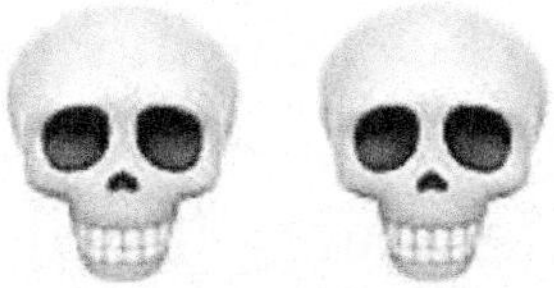

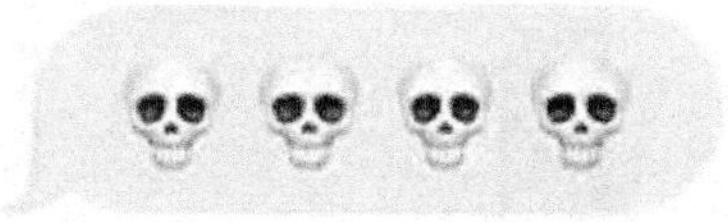

The emoji selector has also been upgraded by Apple. The emoji window now has more room between them, bigger emoji, and the Sticker and Memoji interfaces built right in.

To access Memoji and Stickers, tap on the corresponding icons on the emoji picker's bottom left. From the two tabs on the emoji picker, you may build new stickers and Memojis. Go to the sticker area and hit the blank sticker button to make a new sticker. Press the three dots in the upper right corner of the Memoji screen to access the menu where you may choose New, Edit, or Duplicate.

HOW TO USE MEMOJI AND STICKERS AS EMOJI

Because you may now use a sticker or Memoji exactly like an emoji, the emoji picker now has new specific areas for each. For instance, when you insert a sticker into your text while typing, it will be appended to the end of your text instead of delivered as an individual picture.

If you want to send a full-size sticker but don't want to include text, you may still do so.

The following operating systems are required to show stickers and memes transmitted as emojis: iOS 18, iPadOS 18, macOS Sequoia, visionOS 2, and watchOS 11. As in previous iOS versions, stickers are still transmitted as individual photos.

HOW TO USE TEXT FORMATTING

With the additional formatting choices, you can make your text messages even better. When you're done typing, hit the "A" button up there. You may now format anything you've written as bold, italic, underlined, or strikethrough because it is chosen.

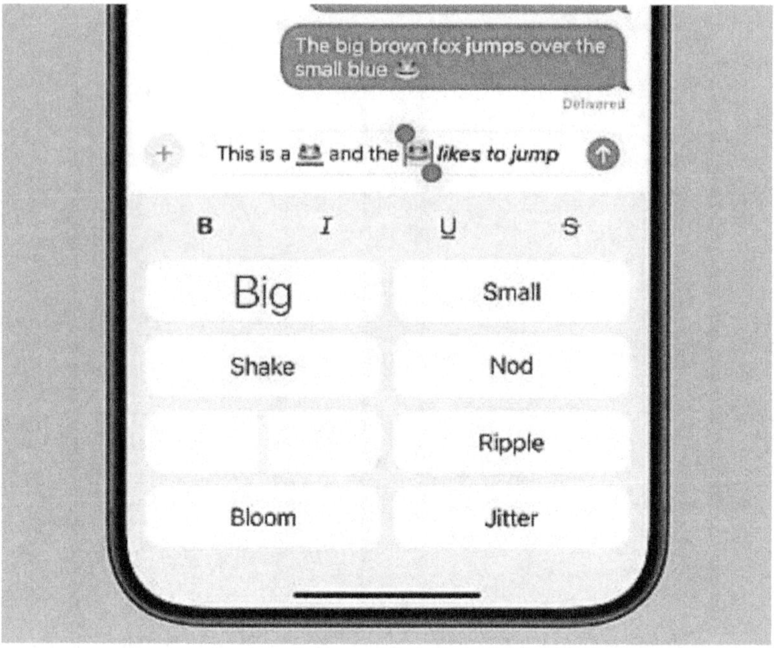

Pressing the "A" symbol after double-tapping a word will allow you to apply formatting to just that word. The pop-up menu also has the Text Effects option, which you may use. Even though emojis support formatting, the bold and italic styles have no effect.

You may now add additional dynamic text effects to your whole message, a single word, a sentence, or even an emoji or sticker, in addition to the standard formatting options like bold, italic, underline, and strikethrough.

HOW TO USE MESSAGES WITH TEXT EFFECTS

After double-tapping the text you want to modify, you may access the text effects interface by tapping the "A" symbol.

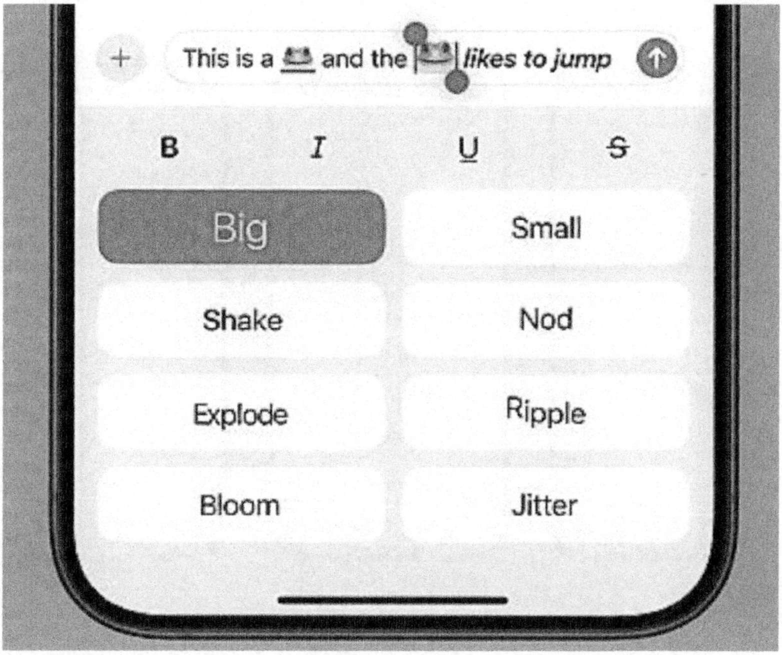

Any text or emoji with an effect applied will keep animating when seen in a chat with someone running iOS 18 or one of its sibling releases. You won't see these effects or be able to use them on prior Apple operating systems.

HOW TO USE MATH NOTES

You may use the built-in Math Notes function in Messages to have your iPhone answer problems. Enter an equation to see it in action; the addition of an equals sign will immediately provide the solution.

If you're using the Messages app to convert between different units of measurement, temperatures, currencies, and more, Math Notes will function just fine. Simply enter your desired conversion, such as "20 euros to dollars," and then add an equals sign to get the answer.

HOW TO LINK CARD UPDATE

The Messages app's link cards now include colorful backgrounds that harmonize with the color of the primary picture in the link—if one is present—thanks to a redesign by Apple.

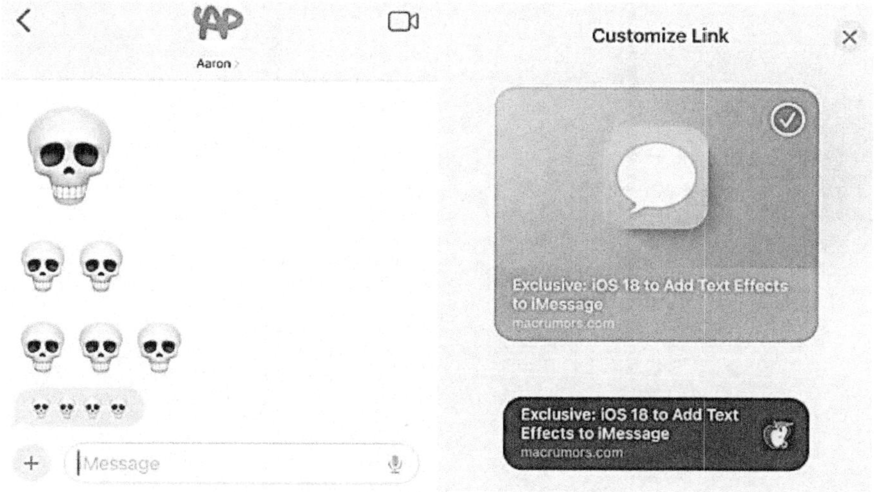

Just before sending a link, you may see a preview of it. Long pressing gives you choices to personalize it. Converting a link card to a more basic card layout or turning it into a text link that displays the hyperlink alone, without any preview, is also an option.

HOW TO USE PICTURE PLAYGROUND

Like other artificial intelligence picture-generating platforms, the soon-to-be-released Apple Intelligence feature called Picture Playground will allow you to generate images using text-based instructions.

If you want to make and send photographs without leaving the Messages app, you can now do so with the help of Apple's Image Playground. Using the text you enter into the Messages app, Apple Intelligence may deduce the main points of your discussion and provide picture choices.

With Image Playground, you can even include photos of your loved ones—so the next time you're talking with a pal, you can make a funny picture using their contact photo. There is no way to create a picture that would pass for a genuine one since Apple applies a style to everyone.

All picture creation happens on the spot, and you have your pick of animation, illustration, and sketch styles.

HOW TO USE THE APPLE INTELLIGENCE GENMOJI

Genmoji, which is based on Image Playground, provides a text prompt for creating personalized emoji. Is an ice cream cone with mint chocolate chips something you've always desired as an emoji? You can make it with Genmoji.

Do you need an unusual flower that isn't a rose or a sunflower, or maybe a pizza-based cat? With Genmoji, it's within reach. You may use the Genmoji UI to define a Genmoji and have many suggestions generated by Apple Intelligence.

Like Image Playground, you can even use a friend's or family member's contact image to make an emoji.

You may use emojis instead of emojis since they act and look exactly like emojis.

Notes: Any model of iPhone 16, including the 15 Pro and 15 Pro Max, will be required to access the future Apple Intelligence capabilities in iOS 18 and subsequent versions. Apple Intelligence is also compatible with Macs and iPads from the M-series.

CHAPTER FIVE

HOW TO USE SIRI ON IOS 18

Use just your voice to do commonplace chores. Siri has several useful functions, such as phrase translation, alarm setting, location finding, weather reporting, and online knowledge summarization.

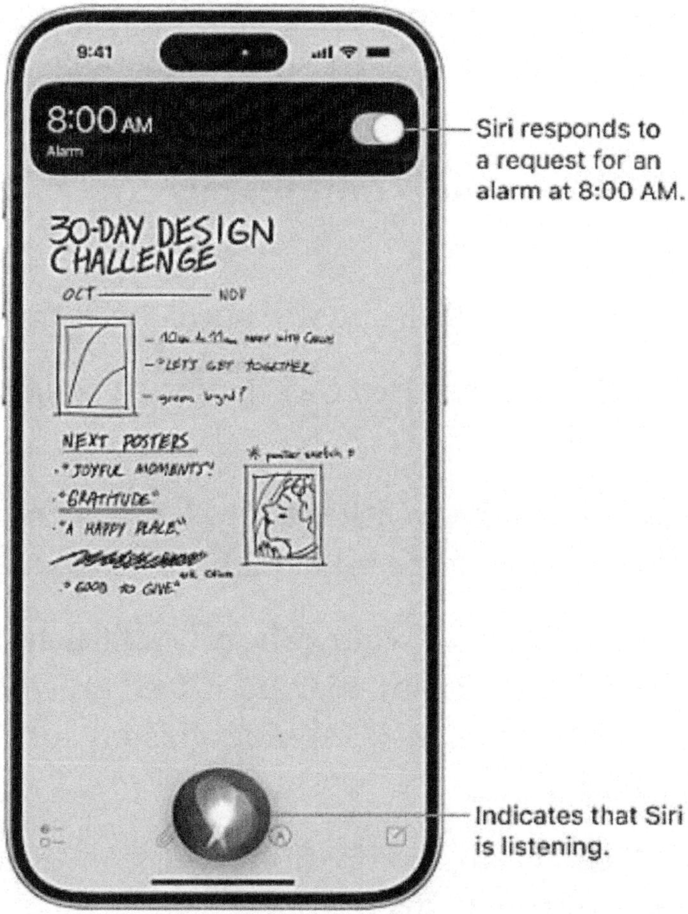

HOW TO SET UP SIRI

Following these steps will enable Siri if it wasn't already there when you first set up your iPhone:

1) To access Talk to Siri, go to Settings > Siri.

2) To access Siri, choose "Hey Siri" or just "Siri" (if available).

Note: In some languages and areas, you may get the option to say just "Siri" on compatible iPhone models.

How To Use Voice Commands To Activate Siri

When you speak to Siri, she will speak back to you.

Just call out "Siri" or "Hey Siri" and then speak your query or request.

"Hey Siri, what's the weather for today?" is one such scenario. An alarm to go off at eight in the morning

Tip: You may turn off your iPhone's ability to react to "Siri" or "Hey Siri" by placing it face down or by going to Settings > Siri, tapping "Listen for," and then selecting Off.

If your AirPods are compatible, you can also use your voice to launch Siri.

HOW TO ACTIVATE SIRI WITH A BUTTON

If your iPhone is in silent mode, you may still use the button to activate Siri, and she will react quietly. Siri speaks her responses aloud when quiet mode is disabled.

1) Pick one option out of these:

- iPhone With Face ID: Press and hold down the side button.
- iPhone That Has A Physical Home button: Press and hold the Home Button.
- EarPods: Press the center or call button.
- CarPlay: either press and hold the wheel-mounted voice command button or the Home button on the CarPlay Home Screen.
- Use Siri Eyes Free: Just press and hold the wheel-mounted voice command button.

2) Make a request or ask a question.

To illustrate, you may ask, "What is 18 percent of 225?" or "Turn the clock backward three minutes."

Additionally, compatible AirPods allow you to summon Siri with a simple tap.

Request Things In A Sequential Order

You don't have to turn Siri off and then back on again to make follow-up queries.

1) Start Siri going, and then ask for something.
2) It would be appreciated if you could submit another request right away.

Interrupting Siri mid-sentence will force it to stop responding to your request.

"Hey Siri, could you tell me the San Francisco weather?" Is Cupertino still an option?

Make A Correction If Siri Misunderstands You

- As you make consecutive requests: Please restate your request using new wording.
- If your requests aren't consecutive, try tapping the Listen button and then rephrasing your question.
- Give more details about what you want: If Siri misunderstood your request, try spelling them out again after tapping the Listen button. For instance, after saying "Call," spell out the name of the individual.
- Edit communication before transmission: Call for a replacement.
- If your request is shown onscreen, you may make textual edits to it. Follow the on-screen keyboard prompts after tapping the request.

Tip: Substitute the revised request for the first one right after it to avoid having to activate Siri again. (Only certain nations and regions' supported iPhone models are eligible.)

Type Instead Of Talking To Siri

1) Accessibility > Siri in the Settings menu allows you to enable Type to Siri.
2) Launch Siri, then put in your query or request using the keyboard and text box.

HOW TO USE SIRI TO ANSWER QUESTIONS

Quickly verify information, do computations, or translate phrases into many languages with Siri. Attract Siri's attention and then say:

- "How does a rainbow form?"
- "Could you tell me how a cat sounds?"
- The derivative of cosine x, may I ask?
- "Who was the inventor of the first rocket to reach orbit?"
- "What is the Mandarin word for 'thank you?'"

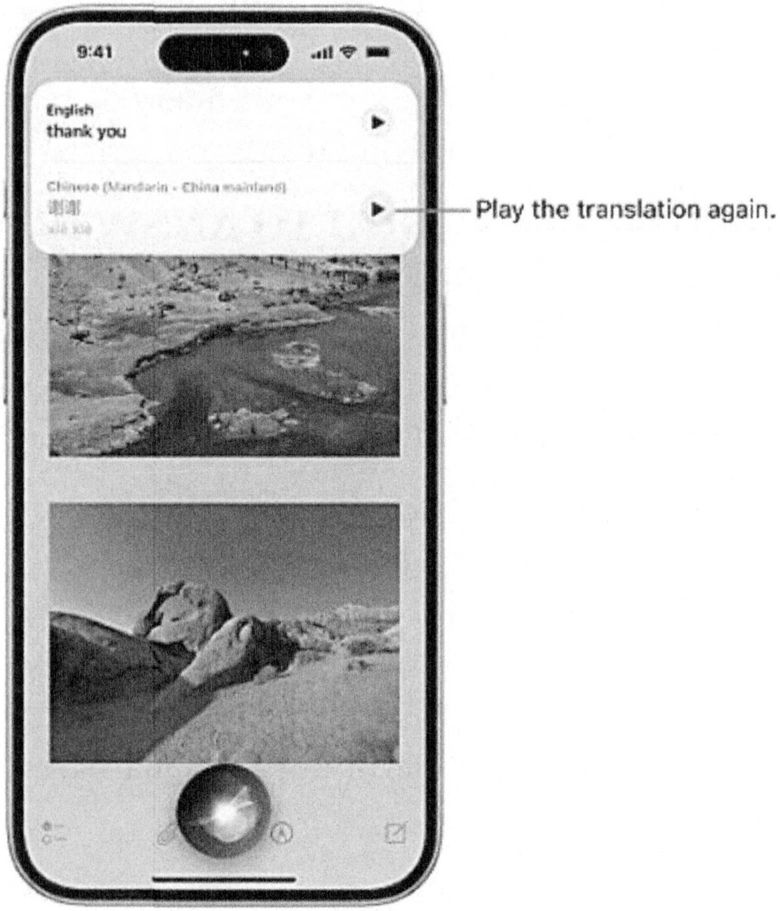

USE Siri With Other Applications

Voice commands are now possible with the help of Siri. When you want to use Siri, just say:

- Requesting a meeting with Gordon at 9 to add it to the calendar.

- Select "Artichokes" from the list of items to be added to Reminders.
- Put "Send a message to PoChun saying love you heart emoji" into your Messages to type out your message.
- "Regarding my status, what has changed?" to stay up-to-date on local weather conditions, current events, news, reminders, and more.

MAKE USE OF SIRI TO COMMUNICATE WITH OTHERS

Contacts may be notified of on-screen elements including images, websites, Apple Music or Podcasts content, Maps locations, and more.

Just activate Siri when viewing a picture in your library and say "Send this to mom" to compose a fresh message using the photo.

HOW TO UPDATE APPS ON THE IOS 18

With each iOS update, the pre-installed apps on your iPhone get the latest versions. You may choose to manually update an app or have it updated automatically when you download it from the App Store.

Disable Automatic App Updates

1) Navigate to the App Store under Settings.
2) You may disable app updates.

Update App Manually

1) On your iPhone, launch the App Store.
2) Select "My Account" or tap your profile image in the upper right.
3) Select the applications you want to update by scrolling down and tapping Update next to them, or select Update All.

Following an update, the app will be added to the list of applications located below Updated Recently.

COMMON PROBLEMS AND SOLUTIONS ON IOS 18

Battery Drain

Issues with power depletion are one of the less desirable aspects of iOS 18. There are primarily two explanations for this. The first is that iOS 18's new features aren't yet ready for prime time, and the second is that there's a continuous diagnostic procedure and data transmission going on to make iOS 18 better in the end.

Follow these steps to resolve the issues:

- Restart your iPhone.
- Go into the settings and disable the option to reload the program in the background.
- Adjust brightness.

Overheating Phone

Even when used normally, some iPhone owners have complained that the gadget is too heavy. This means that the device's hardware isn't compatible with anything. Problems like the iPhone overheating may arise even when doing simple things like navigating through social networking applications, viewing movies offline, or talking if the operating system isn't suited for the device's hardware.

- Restart your iPhone.
- When you're not using an app, you should close it from the recent applications menu.
- Keep your iPhone out of the sun.
- Remove the rear case as a solution.

When Your iPhone Is Laggy

Your iPhone is not alone if it has become slow and clumsy while using light applications. There must be enough space on the smartphone to install the latest iOS 18 update. In regular usage, a device that is overloaded with data could seem slow and unresponsive.

- Restart your iPhone.
- When you're not using an app, you should close it from the recent applications menu.
- Keep your iPhone out of the sun.
- Remove the rear case as a solution.

IOS 18 Not Showing For Update

Users are seeing mixed reactions to the iOS 18 upgrade; some are finding the update in the settings, while others are reporting issues after downloading the update. In most cases, you can find the most recent iOS update under the Settings menu, then go to General, and finally Software Updates on your iPhone.

If the new iOS 18 update isn't visible, it's because you haven't registered for the program. Apple only notifies iPhone users who have requested the upgrade. The following procedures may be followed to apply for the iOS 18 update:

- The first thing you need do is enroll in the Apple Software Program.
- After tapping on Open Updates, choose the Open option.

- After that, you'll be able to check which version of iOS 18 is compatible with your smartphone. Choose iOS 18 and save it to your computer.

CHAPTER SIX

TIPS AND TRICKS

No one is more confused than you are about what to do after installing the most recent iOS 18 update on your iPhone. To get you started, here are 18 recommendations for operating systems:

1) Change Your Home Screen

With the release of iOS 18, Apple has finally made it possible to manipulate the widgets and icons on the home screen, giving you complete control over what you see. You have complete freedom to alter the color, size, and placement of your icons right from the off, and you can even make your custom widgets to make common tasks easier.

This may be accomplished by pressing and holding the home screen until the 'Edit' option appears in the upper left corner. If you wish to change the look of your home screen, tap that. To toggle between bright and dark themes, you'll find a slider with tint choices and other features. Plus, you may coordinate your icons with your one-of-a-kind background if you so like.

2) Personalize Your Lock Screen

Another revamped feature is the ability to customize shortcuts right from your iPhone's lock screen. If you're sick and tired of inadvertently turning on your iPhone flashlight, you can change it with a shortcut that you like. With this one, you're not limited to just activating dark mode or making your iPhone become an Apple TV controller.

3) Adjust Your Torch

When we talk about the flashlight, we should mention that Apple has made some great new adjustments so you may personalize it. Through the iPhone's Dynamic Island, you can use the new flashlight option and adjust the brightness to suit your requirements. Altering the light's distribution across a broad or limited region is also possible with a horizontal swipe.

4) Modify Your Control Center

Now that iOS 18 is out, the Control Centre is much better than before. You may rearrange the grids, add or delete tools, and make as many control sheets as you like. Swiping into the Control Centre and tapping the + symbol in the upper left corner will do the trick.

You may use this to change the icons already there or add new ones. You have the option to resize and rearrange them as you choose.

5) Hide Or Lock Your Applications

Users may now lock or hide applications from the home screen in iOS 18. When you hide an app, it will only be available via the Hidden Applications folder and will not be shown in searches or alerts. Additionally, for added security, you have the option to open them with your Face ID, Touch ID, or password.

6) Familiarize Yourself With The Calculator App

At long last, the calculator app has a delete option! However, iOS 18 introduces even more changes. First, Apple has introduced Math Notes, a fantastic alternative to Calculator that combines the best features of both apps. When you enter an equal to sign into Math Notes, the app will automatically answer your problems.

Even inside the Calculator app, iOS 18 streamlines unit conversions. This allows you to do metric conversions like distance, currency, and more without ever leaving the app. Finally, the three lines in the upper left of the interface allow you to view the Calculator history.

7) Make A Wi-Fi QR Code

Although there are some options, iOS 18 makes it even easier by allowing you to create a custom QR code to share your home Wi-Fi network. By selecting Wi-Fi from inside the Passwords app, you can see all of your stored Wi-Fi networks, including your current connection, at the top of the list.

After that, give it a touch. Then, on the subsequent page, choose the "Show Network QR code" option.

You should be able to establish a network connection by scanning it using a different phone.

8) Satellite Messages

Have to message someone but can't connect to the internet? Those with an iPhone 14 or later may now use the emergency feature in iOS 18 to send a text message via satellite. You may use this function, which is an expansion of Emergency SOS, to send and receive text messages with all the capabilities that support them. We doubt that you'll ever require emoji tapbacks with your satellite messages when stuck on a highway, but they are still an option!

9) Establish Charge Limit

Setting and customizing charge restriction duration is now possible with iOS 18. The basic premise was that the gadget will extend the life of your iPhone's battery if you don't always charge it to full capacity.

In contrast to earlier software versions, iOS 18 allows you to adjust the restriction in five percent increments. Find Charging in the Settings menu, after which go to Battery.

The next page should allow you to specify restrictions, ranging from eighty percent to one hundred percent. Along with learning your routines, iOS 18 will also be able to tailor suggestions to your specific iPhone use.

After you've decided on a limit, you may set it by tapping the "Set Charge Limit" button. Now when you put it in, it will charge up to the limit you choose, not to full capacity.

10) Use The Action Button To Find Music

Apple brought in the Action button last year and today the possibilities to customize it seem endless. With the iOS 18 update, you can replace your regular function with Shazam to discover new music around you. Earlier versions of the software would only allow you to do this using the shortcuts app; however, Apple now gives you a direct way to use Shazam.

Printed in Great Britain
by Amazon

49496281R00086